Saving the Sarus Crane

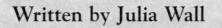

Written by Julia Wall

Vietnam

My name is Huy. I live in Ho Chi Minh City, Vietnam. I have never seen a sarus crane, but I hope that one day there will be thousands of these beautiful birds in my country. Do you know why there are hardly any sarus cranes left?

Contents

Look for the **Activity Zone!**
When you see this picture, you will find
an activity to try.

The Tallest Flying Birds

Sarus cranes are the world's tallest flying birds. Some male sarus cranes reach six feet tall, which is taller than many adult humans. There are three kinds of sarus cranes; the kind found in Vietnam, Laos, and Cambodia is called the *eastern sarus crane*.

In Vietnam, sarus cranes are the symbol of long life and happy families. They disappeared during the Vietnam War (1957–1975), when much of their habitat was destroyed. For many years, people thought that the cranes were gone forever. Then, in 1984, Vietnamese scientists reported the discovery of a small flock.

Pointed bill for catching fish

Large wings—from tip to tip, the wingspan is 8 feet.

habitat   the place where an animal or plant lives

4

Birds need to be light to fly. Although sarus cranes are as tall as an adult human, they only weigh as much as a six-month-old baby.

Sarus cranes have gray feathers, or plumage, and red necks and heads.

Long legs for wading in shallow water

What Is Ornithology?

The word *ornithology* means "the scientific study of birds." Scientists who study birds are called *ornithologists*. Some ornithologists study birds in the wild; others work in zoos or wildlife parks. Some teach people about birds or write books and research papers about them.

Families on the Move

In Vietnam, the sarus crane's breeding grounds have all been destroyed. Radio-tracking studies show that sarus cranes breed in Laos and northern Cambodia during the rainy season, which lasts from May to November. In the cooler dry season, they migrate to wetlands in the Mekong Delta in Vietnam and southern Cambodia, where there is plenty of food.

When a male sarus crane wants to attract a female, he does a kind of dance. This might involve jumping, running, flapping his wings, and throwing grass and feathers into the air. Later, he will help the female protect her eggs and keep them warm.

migrate   to travel to different places at different times of the year

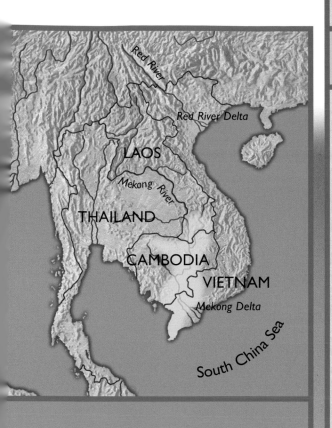

The yellow part of this map shows the habitat of the eastern sarus crane.

Sarus cranes are strong fliers with good eyesight, often traveling 1–2 miles above the ground. They usually fly in a line or in a V-shape, a formation in which some birds follow other birds and save energy by not having to push aside as much air.

Nest Building

Sarus cranes need large, open areas with plenty of vegetation for building their nests. Once nest building starts, a pair will chase away other birds that want to nest nearby. Their eggs hatch after 28–35 days. The chicks are a yellow-brown color.

Male and female sarus cranes pair for life, and they return to the same breeding grounds year after year.

Water-Filled Wetlands

Sarus cranes live in areas that are mostly covered in shallow water. These places are called *wetlands*, and they include swamps, marshes, and river deltas.

Many people used to think that this kind of land was useless, and the water in many wetlands was drained away so that the land could be used for farming. However, people now know that wetlands help control flooding and provide homes for many of the world's rarest animals, including many species of water birds.

delta   the area at the mouth of a river, just before it joins the sea, where it fans out and becomes wide and shallow

Conserving wetlands around the world is a matter of international importance. If a water bird's habitat is destroyed in one country, that species will no longer be found in any of the other countries that it migrates to.

Wetland Diets

Wetlands are full of the kinds of foods that water birds depend on, including fish, frogs, insects, and plankton, which are very tiny animals and plants that can be seen only with a microscope. Eastern sarus cranes eat a wide variety of plants and animals that need the special conditions present in wetlands to survive. Their diet includes grasses, worms, and frogs.

Habitats in Danger

Eastern sarus cranes depend on wetlands for food, water, and shelter. However, their habitats are in danger, because many wetland areas have been turned into rice paddies to feed Vietnam's growing population. There are also other threats to sarus crane habitats. For instance, human-made canals sometimes raise water levels so that they are too high for grasses to grow. Fertilizers that are used to grow rice and chemicals that are used to kill insects cause pollution in wetland areas. Additionally, the sarus crane population is threatened by poachers, who illegally catch the birds and use them for food or sell them to collectors.

The Vietnamese people eat mainly rice. Rice crops grow only in fields covered in fresh, gently flowing water.

Because the eastern sarus crane faces so many threats, it is now endangered. Scientists estimate that there are probably only 500 to 1,500 left. The population will continue to decrease unless more action is taken to save it.

endangered an animal that could die out because so few are left

The Vietnamese government has set up six areas to protect Vietnam's wildlife and is working to establish more. Because many tourists want to visit these places, roads have now been built into many of these remote areas. Unfortunately, better access means that it is easier for hunters and poachers to damage populations and habitats. It is important that people are educated about conservation and that enough money is available to pay people to protect the wildlife.

Saving the Sarus Crane

To save the eastern sarus crane, scientists believe the following actions need to be priorities.

- Expand research on eastern sarus cranes (where they live, what they need, how they behave, etc.).
- Do more research on wetlands so that they can be managed in the best possible way.
- Restore and protect existing sarus crane habitats.
- Make sure that rice growing will have the least possible effect on sarus crane habitats.
- Educate farmers about wetland plants and animals and how they can help the environment.
- Teach schoolchildren about the threats that sarus cranes face and what people can do to help.

priority   something considered particularly important

The whooping crane of North America is related to the sarus crane. However, it is even rarer. There are fewer than 400 whooping cranes left.

If Vietnamese schoolchildren know about sarus cranes, they will be able to teach others in their families. When they grow up, they might make decisions that help save the cranes.

Activity Zone!

The sarus crane is only one of many birds that need our help. Find out which rare birds live near you. Pick one and find out the following.

- What sort of place does it live in (wetlands, forest, shore, etc.)?

- What does it eat?

- Where, if anywhere, does it migrate?

- Where does it nest?

- Why is it in danger?

- What can people do to help?

Write a letter to the editor of a local newspaper or to a children's television show. Explain about the birds and why they need help. You might even have some suggestions about what people can do to help.

The Mekong Delta

The Mekong Delta covers about ten million acres of southern Vietnam as well as parts of other countries. It is where eastern sarus cranes spend the winter, or dry season. Several reserves have been set up in the area to protect the wetland ecosystems.

Ornithologists have counted 92 species of water birds living in the Mekong Delta in Vietnam. This list includes large populations of herons, egrets, storks, and ibises, which nest in huge groups, or colonies, in the forests and mangrove swamps. Thousands of acres of trees have been replanted, and the Ministry of Forestry wants to increase the number even further.

The Mekong Delta is popular not only with birds; more than 50 percent of the people in southern Vietnam live in this area.

ecosystem   animals, plants, and their environment

The Asian openbill stork is another water bird that lives in the Mekong Delta. Its long, pointed bill is perfect for catching fish and for pulling creatures such as crabs out of the mud.

Wetland Food Web

Bird colonies can help the people living in the surrounding areas. Many birds feed on insects and other pests that attack rice crops. Also, bird droppings help produce plankton, which feed the shrimp and fish that people eat.

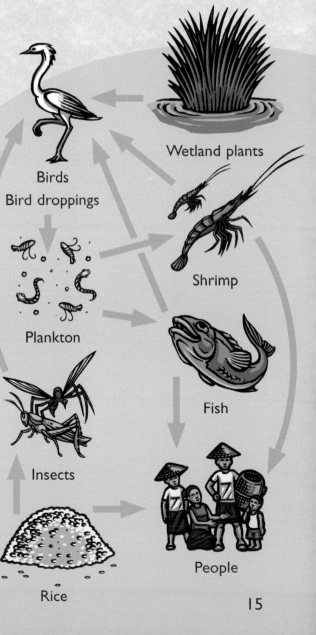

Wetland plants

Birds
Bird droppings

Shrimp

Plankton

Fish

Insects

People

Rice

Tram Chim National Park

The eastern sarus crane was first rediscovered in an area of Tram Chim National Park in 1984. The park has more than 600 sarus cranes, the largest number in the Mekong Delta. Since 1985, it has been protected so that the cranes will continue to migrate there each winter.

Eastern sarus cranes can find their favorite food at Tram Chim National Park—the Chinese water chestnut. However, the marshlands where this chestnut grows have decreased from 2,500 to 500 acres because of rice production and shrimp farming. The cranes' habitat is also threatened by forest fires.

Wardens at Tram Chim National Park take fishing nets from local people who fish there illegally. It is important that enough fish are available for the cranes and other rare birds.

The Chinese water chestnut grows in shallow water. This grasslike plant has round, underground stems, called *corms*, which are eaten by both animals and people.

Flower

Leaves

Corm

Roots

Tram Chim National Park is part of a large wetland area in the Mekong Delta. It used to be covered in thick vegetation and small streams, but most of it is now used to grow rice. During the rainy season, it becomes a huge lake, with some areas flooding to nearly 12 feet deep. In the photo above, the security chief, Than Hoang Dan, watches for the return of the cranes at the start of the dry season.

Tram Chim National Park may become a Ramsar Site. This is a wetland of international importance with endangered habitats.

Hats and Habitats

In 1998, a new site where eastern sarus cranes spend the winter was discovered. It is a 1,000-acre area of grassland at Hon Chong, part of the Mekong River Delta in Vietnam. Farmers are being taught how to harvest grass in this area without harming the environment, so the sarus cranes will be protected.

The harvested grass is used to make items such as hats and handbags, which are sold in nearby Ho Chi Minh City. This project is called *Ha Tien: Habitats and Handbags*. It helps protect the land and provides incomes for many families living near the wetlands.

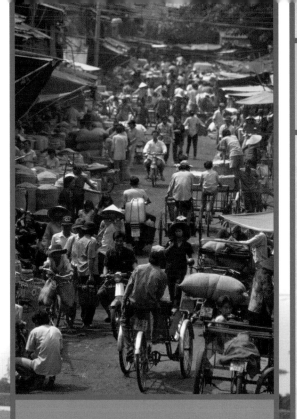

Ho Chi Minh City is the largest city in Vietnam. Locally produced goods, such as foods and crafts, are sold in the city's many open-air markets.

Scientists group animals into categories that tell us how close to extinction they are. The most serious category is *critical*. Two slightly less serious categories are *endangered* and *threatened*.

The White-Shouldered Ibis

Hon Chong also provides a habitat for other rare birds, such as the white-shouldered ibis. This wading bird is critically close to extinction, with only 50 to 250 birds left worldwide. It has lost most of its feeding and nesting areas, because trees have been cut down, and the wetlands have been used for growing rice. The white-shouldered ibis will need a lot of protection to survive.

The Red River Delta

The Red River Delta is in northern Vietnam. It has many wetlands and coastal habitats where some bird species breed and others stop over on their way from Siberia to Australia.

Seventy-eight species of birds have been recorded on the delta, and twelve of these are threatened, including the black-headed ibis and the black-faced spoonbill. This is because people are converting more acres into farmland and because people are taking so many mollusks and crabs from along the coast that there are not enough left for foraging birds, such as the black-faced spoonbill.

Black-headed ibis

forage to search a large area for food

These boys are setting fish traps in canals among the rice paddies. The fish will be used to flavor rice dishes. Although growing rice uses up valuable land, it takes up less space than wheat, corn, or animal farms. Nevertheless, it is important to find ways to grow rice while at the same time protecting wildlife.

Xuan Thang Wildlife Reserve

There are only about 800 black-faced spoonbills left. About 200 of them spend their winters at the Xuan Thang Wildlife Reserve on the Red River Delta. The reserve provides much-needed habitats for these and other water birds. It has three major wetland habitats:

- canals and rivers
- coastal mud flats, mangrove swamps, salt marshes, and sandy beaches
- large islands

Action is being taken to increase the number of reserve staff, encourage farmers not to use harmful pesticides or fertilizers, and stop new rice paddies from being created.

pesticide a chemical used to kill animals that harm crops

More About Water Birds

River deltas and coastlines make up much of Vietnam's land, and many of the birds that live there are water birds. There are water birds in most other countries as well. They live on ocean beaches, lake shores, and by almost every river, stream, and pond.

Most water birds feed on fish, shrimp, crabs, and other tiny water creatures. Many of them have specially shaped beaks that help them catch food. Some have webbed feet to help them swim. Wetland birds often have long legs for wading in shallow water.

Hooked beak

Long neck

Flamingos are wading birds. Some live in fresh water and others in salt water. They use their hooked beaks to scoop up muddy water containing insects and tiny shellfish.

Webbed foot

Long, thin legs

Pelicans have a soft pouch in the underside of their bills. They use their bill like a net to scoop up fish near the surface of the water.

Bird watching is a hobby that anyone can take up, even city dwellers. A good place to start is a local park, lake, or wildlife center. If you go bird watching, remember to do the following.

- Take a notebook to write about the birds you see.
- Take along a book of local birds for identifying unknown birds.
- Take binoculars and a camera if you have them.
- Ask a trusted adult to go with you.

When recording notes about a bird, observe the following things.

Wing markings

Eye markings

Beaks

Legs and feet

Find Out More!

1. What are some endangered water birds in your country, and what is being done to help them?

2. Plan a class visit to a bird conservation place in your local area, and find out what you can do to help.

To find out more about the ideas in *Saving the Sarus Crane*, visit **www.researchit.org** on the web.

Index